12/04

UNIVERSITY OF
WOLVERHAMPTON

Harrison Learning Centre
City Campus
University of Wolverhampton
St Peter's Square
Wolverhampton WV1 1RH
Telephone: 0845 408 1631

2 4 MAR 2010		
17		

Telephone Renewals: 01902 321333
Please RETURN this item on or before the last date shown above.
Fines will be charged if items are returned late.
See tariff of fines displayed at the Counter (L2)

£ 1.20

Introduction to the study of revolutions and some interpretations of 1848

Prepared by Clive Emsley and Ursula Semin for the Course Team

The Open University Press

Clive Emsley is Lecturer in History at The Open University.

Ursula Semin is Research Administrator at the Richardson Institute for Conflict
and Peace Research.

The Open University Press
Walton Hall, Milton Keynes
MK7 6AA

First published 1976

Designed by the Media Development Group of The Open University.

PRINTED IN GREAT BRITAIN BY
EYRE AND SPOTTISWOODE LIMITED AT
GROSVENOR PRESS, PORTSMOUTH.

ISBN 0 335 05050 6

This text forms part of an Open University course. The complete list of units in the course
appears at the end of this text.

For general availability of supporting material referred to in this text, please write to the Director
of Marketing, The Open University, P.O. Box 81, Walton Hall, Milton Keynes, MK7 6AT.

Further information on Open University courses may be obtained from the Admissions Office,
The Open University, P.O. Box 48, Walton Hall, Milton Keynes, MK7 6AB.

1.1

CONTENTS UNIT 1

1.1 GENERAL AIMS AND OVERALL PLAN OF THE COURSE

It is not a bad thing at the very beginning for teachers to spell out what they hope their students will be able to do as a result of completing a course. Given the specific Open University problem of teaching at a distance, such a statement at the beginning is perhaps even more valuable than in a conventional teaching situation. In this course on the Revolutions of 1848 the course team have four general aims:

1 To enable you to develop skills in the handling and interpreting of historical source material and in the writing of history.

2 To enable you to analyse and assess the importance of the events of 1848.

3 To enable you to discuss critically and informedly the four following themes in relation to the revolutions of 1848:

   (a) the causes of the revolutions.
   (b) who participated (and, of course, who did not participate) in the revolutions, at what stage, and why.
   (c) the results, both short-term and long-term, of the revolutions.
   (d) how the revolutions were interpreted by contemporaries, and how, subsequently, they have been interpreted by historians.

4 To enable you to consider some of the problems involved in the relationship between the historical events of 1848 and developments in literature, music and art.

Perhaps the first of these aims seems a little formidable or pompous, but Arthur Marwick's notes on the writing of history in this course which accompany this unit will explain our intentions fully. Apart from this, I think that these general aims are self-explanatory.

The course has been planned in four parts of four units each:

Part I	Unit 1	Introduction to the study of revolutions and some interpretations of 1848
	Unit 2	Europe on the eve of 1848
	Unit 3	Document collection
	Unit 4	*Sentimental Education*: a Study Guide
Part II	**France 1848–1851**	
	Unit 5	France, February–December 1848
	Unit 6	France, January 1849–December 1851
	Unit 7	Interpretation of the French Revolution: Karl Marx and Alexis de Tocqueville
	Unit 8	Art in the French Revolution
Part III	**Germany, Austria and Italy**	
	Unit 9	Revolutions in Germany
	Unit 10	Revolutions in the Austrian Empire
	Unit 11	Revolutions in Italy
	Unit 12	Music and revolution: Verdi
Part IV	Unit 13	Flaubert's *Sentimental Education*
	Unit 14	Britain and Ireland in the 1840s
	Unit 15	
	Unit 16	Surveys and themes (a collection of essays by members of the course team covering aspects of the revolutions only briefly touched upon elsewhere in the course).

As you will see, we have attempted to make the first three units in each part a solid piece of historical work and, following the old maxim that a change is as good as a rest, make the fourth unit a different discipline study which, nevertheless, relates closely to what has gone before. In Part II for example, after three units of an in-depth study of the revolution in France, you will be studying the effect of that revolution upon French art.

In this opening part you will see that Unit 3 is a collection of documents; these documents have been selected by the authors of the different course units and you will be expected to study them in detail with the units to which they relate. Ostensibly then there is no work set for you in Unit 3; however, we have devised a particularly heavy work-load for Unit 2 and you will certainly need to spread your work on this unit into the time you would have allotted for Unit 3. Apart from this, I believe that the plan, like the general aims, is fairly straightforward.

Besides the overall strategy contained in the general aims of the course, each unit has its own particular objectives relating to those aims. Aside from this general introduction to the course this unit has two aims:

1   to introduce you to the study of revolutions in general
2   to introduce you to some of the different historical interpretations of 1848.

You will require one of your set books for Section 1.4 of this unit: Melvin Kranzberg, *1848: A Turning Point?*

The first radio programme in this course is directly related to Sections 1.2 and 1.3 of this unit. You should read these sections carefully before listening to the programme.

1.2   REVOLUTION AS A SUBJECT FOR STUDY

In this section I shall look at some of the questions surrounding the study of revolutions mainly from an historian's point of view. In Section 1.3, Ursula Semin will examine how social scientists have studied revolutions. The two sections overlap, of course, since History and Social Science are not mutually exclusive disciplines, but the difference in technique and aim should be apparent.

(Some of the questions which we discuss below have also been examined in Block 3 of the Second Level Social Science Course 'Comparative Government and Politics'.[1] If you have taken that course you may wish to turn again to the relevant discussion especially in Units 11–12.)

1.2.1   SOME INITIAL PROBLEMS

The word 'revolution' slips very easily off the pen, or off the tongue, in the contemporary world. As Arthur Marwick noted in *The Nature of History*, 'historians are very free in their use of the word, detecting educational revolutions, scientific revolutions, social revolutions, and even historical revolutions'.[2]

---

[1] The Open University (1974) D231 Comparative Government, The Open University Press.

[2] Arthur Marwick, *The Nature of History*, Macmillan, 1970, p. 166, A100 set book.

Of course historians are not the only people who use the word, and not the only people to complicate its definition. In his collection of readings called *Revolution*, Krishan Kumar gave

> a brief recital of some of the many uses of the word 'revolution' [which, he believed] should sufficiently shake any complacency that might exist as to the complexity of the problem. We have the French Revolution, the Freudian Revolution, the Scientific Revolution, the Industrial Revolution, the Managerial Revolution, the Greek Revolution (in artistic development), the Technological Revolution, the Student Revolution. Nor is the chaos contained by any firm commitment to a temporal span within which the alleged revolution has to happen. Two anthropologists, Hockett and Ascher, speak of 'the human revolution', that 'drastic set of changes that turned non-humans into humans'. These drastic changes, they agree, 'may have required a good many millions of years; yet they can validly be regarded as sudden in view of the tens of millions of years of mammalian history that preceded them'. . . . Today, our journalists write of revolutions occurring annually, sometimes monthly and weekly, in describing the succession of dictatorships in Latin America, the Middle East and Africa. (Krishan Kumar, *Revolution: The Theory and Practice of a European Idea*, Weidenfeld and Nicholson, 1970, pp. 9–10.)

Yet in spite of all this complexity Kumar believed that it was still possible to make out some family resemblances. 'Revolution' in all of these examples means *change*, and this change is in some sense *fundamental* and *sudden*.

As well as being a commonly used word, 'revolution' can also be an emotive word when used in the context of political, social or even economic change. There have been relatively few socio-political revolutions in human history, but they have generally been dramatic, violent and bloody – events which have caught the eye and excited the passions both at the time and subsequently.

In the first unit of A301, *War and Society*, Arthur Marwick raised the question of whether war was a proper subject for academic study;[3] the same question might be asked of socio-political revolutions (and there have been far fewer such revolutions than wars). Some naïve critics might accuse Arthur Marwick of treating war as 'a good thing' in as much as he has argued that wars can bring about significant social and political changes. While, unlike a war, a revolution aims directly at altering the existing polity, and probably also the existing order of society in a country, historians and anyone else who writes about revolutions, are likely to find themselves being accused similarly of regarding revolution as a 'good' or a 'bad' thing, depending on their interpretation of the significant changes resulting from a revolution. The situation is further complicated by the extreme attitudes adopted towards revolution by persons at the opposite ends of the contemporary political spectrum. Indeed in the introduction to his book *Modern Revolutions* John Dunn asserts that because the basic question raised by revolutions today is so profound – 'do human social conditions *have* to be as unequal and as unjust as everywhere they now are?' – it is a topic about which it is neither possible nor proper to be neutral. Furthermore he considers that 'the value-free study of revolutions is a logical impossibility for those who live in the real world', though he adds the qualification that 'this does not mean that the rational discussion of the values at stake is impossible nor that any prejudice goes'.[4] Now, of course, to point to significant changes arising out of an event as horrible as a war or a bloody

[3] The Open University (1973) A301 *War and Society*, Unit 1 *The Historical Study of War and Society*, The Open University Press, p. 12.

[4] John Dunn, *Modern Revolutions: An Introduction to the Analysis of a Political Phenomenon*, Cambridge University Press, 1972, pp. 1–2 and note 3.

revolution does not signify approval of such phenomena. Wars and revolutions have occurred, and probably will continue to occur in human history; both have brought changes. There is no necessity for the student of either wars or revolutions to seek to excuse or justify excesses, and the conclusions which a student reaches about social and political changes resulting either from wars or revolutions does not necessarily mean that in general he considers wars or revolutions to be either 'good' or 'bad' things. They have occurred; they have had causes and results and as such they are legitimate subjects for historical study.

1.2.2 DEFINITIONS

I mentioned above that Krishan Kumar noted that among the different types of revolutions which he listed it was possible to perceive some kind of family resemblance, namely that these revolutions signified sudden and fundamental change. Given this, you could define the revolutions which we are looking at in this course as 'sudden and fundamental changes in government'; possibly you might add 'changes in society' as well as government. In many respects this definition would be acceptable, but there is, I think, something missing. The definition could, for example, be applicable to the Labour Party's victory in the General Election of 1945 – Labour had an overall majority of 146 and real power in the House of Commons for the first time; tradition has it that one of the new Labour ministers commented, 'We are the masters now!' To take another example from English history, Professor G. R. Elton has written of a Tudor Revolution in government.[5] He argues that during the 1530s, thanks largely to Henry VIII's Secretary Thomas Cromwell ('the most remarkable revolutionary in English history') a modern, national bureaucracy was created in England. Whereas medieval governments were likely to collapse during the reign of a weak king, the bureaucracy created in the 1530s, Elton argues, was capable of functioning and providing political stability, irrespective of the personal qualities of monarchs or their deputies. The Elton thesis has provoked controversy among historians, yet the manner in which Elton has interpreted his material clearly justifies him in speaking of a 'revolution in government'.

Exercise
Obviously neither the Labour Party's victory in 1945, nor the creation of a bureaucracy in the 1530s are revolutions in the style of the great revolutions – England in the 1640s, America in the 1770s and 1780s, France from 1789 (some put it at 1787) to about 1799, Russia in 1917 and, I think it is reasonable to add China in the 1930s and 1940s – though there might be some justification in seeing them as 'revolutions in government'. What elements do you think should be added to my initial definition to make it more specific to the great revolutions?

Discussion
● I think that there are two elements to add: force and mass participation.

The *Oxford English Dictionary* defines political revolution as 'a complete overthrow of the established government in any country by those who were previously subject to it; a forcible substitution of a new ruler or form of government'. The article defining 'revolution' in the *International Encyclopedia of the Social Sciences* also adds this element of force:

[5] G. R. Elton, *The Tudor Revolution in Government*, Cambridge University Press, 1953.

Revolution in its most common sense is an attempt to make a radical change in the system of government. This often involves the infringement of prevailing constitutional arrangements and the use of force.

This article adds that upheaval also requires some popular support; it needs to be transformed into a 'movement' for radical social change, otherwise all you are left with is a *coup d'état* 'in which one ruling clique replaces another, merely substituting one king, colonel or courtier for another, without otherwise affecting the system of government or the fabric of society'.

However, such definitions of revolutions as those I have given above have not gone unchallenged. According to Kumar the trouble is

> not that they do not point to real, identifiable phenomena; but that it is making very poor use of a much more worthwhile concept when revolution is reduced to a mere transfer of power from one group to another.

He sees political revolutions rather as 'interruptions in the pattern of sovereign rule'.

> Political revolution aims to change the style of politics based on the state's monopoly of armed violence. It aims at the dissolution of sovereignty, which is to say, the dissolution of the state. It is in this action that it recognizes political freedom . . . The revolution lasts so long as the monopoly of force is broken, and the organization of social groups is anarchistic. It ends, or is defeated, when one or a number of groups emerges and effectively reconstitutes the sovereign power of the state. This is the counter-revolution, the revolution 'in a reverse direction'. (Kumar, op. cit., pp. 15–16, 27–8, and p. 40.)

Peter Amann gave a similar 'redefinition' in an article in *Political Science Quarterly*. For Amann, who goes on in his article to apply his definition in detail to the events in France during 1848, a revolution is a struggle between a variety of power blocs for dominion after the traditional obedience to an established government has been broken. A power bloc in this context is

> a group, too strong to be suppressed by ordinary police action, which has usurped military, administrative or judicial power traditionally held by the the state. Such a group, defined in terms of its dynamics rather than its organization, may be a highly cohesive para-military formation such as the Nazi S.A. after 1930, an inspired improvization like the workers' councils in the Russian Revolution of 1905 or a completely spontaneous jacquerie. (Peter Amann, 'Revolution: A Redefinition', *Political Science Quarterly* (1962) pp. 39–53.)

Those of you who have taken D231 may recall the more recent and similar definition by Charles Tilly:

> A revolution begins when a government becomes the object of effective, competing, mutually exclusive claims from two or more separate polities. A revolution ends when a single polity – by no means necessarily the same one – regains control over the government. This multiple sovereignty can result from the attempt of one polity to subordinate another heretofore independent polity; from the assertion of sovereignty by a previously subordinate polity; from the formation of a bloc of challengers which seizes control of some portion of the government apparatus; from the fragmentation of an existing polity into blocs, each of which controls some part of the government. (Charles Tilly, 'Does Modernization Breed Revolution?' *Comparative Politics* (1973); reprinted as an offprint in the Supplementary Material for Block 3, D231, Comparative Government, op. cit., p. 32.)

At the beginning of this course I do not necessarily expect you to come down firmly in support of any of these definitions. I have briefly outlined them for

9

you to think about; by and large they can all be said to be applicable to the European revolutions of 1848 which follow in the tradition of the great revolutions.●

1.2.3   CAUSES

Exercise

From your own basic historical knowledge make a list of the general causes of revolutions – it is worth noting down both those causes which you take to be valid, and those which you consider not valid.

Discussion

● Your list may have been something like the following:

(a)   conspiracy and subversion

(b)   a revolutionary ideology

(c)   the appearance of a new and powerful class in society seeking political power equivalent to its new social standing and prominence

(d)   a repressive regime causing discontent

(e)   economic upheaval causing discontent

(f)   serious divisions within the governing class leading to the disintegration of the old regime even before the spark which occasions the revolution.

If you noted more and different causes than these, I hope that I will cover them in the ensuing discussion.

(a) conspiracy and subversion

In his biography of Lord George Bentinck, published just four years after the revolutions of 1848, Disraeli looked back on these upheavals and outlined his own analysis of their causes.

> It was neither parliaments nor populations, nor the course of nature nor the course of events, that overthrew the throne of Louis Philippe. Amid one of those discontents which are appeased by the sacrifice of a favourite or the change of a ministry, the sovereign and the subjects both in confusion, the king deprived of his wonted energy by a prostrating illness and the citizens murmuring without convictions, the throne was surprised by the secret societies, ever prepared to ravage Europe.
>
> The origin of the secret societies that prevail in Europe is very remote. It is probable that they were originally confederations of conquered races organized in a great measure by the abrogated hierarchies. In Italy they have never ceased, although they have at times been obliged to take various forms; sometimes it was a literary academy, sometimes a charitable brotherhood; freemasonry was always a convenient guise. The Inquisition in its great day boasted that it had extirpated them in Spain, but their activity in that country after the first French revolution rather indicates a suspension of vitality than an extinction of life. The reformation gave them a great impulse in Germany, and towards the middle of the eighteenth century, they had not only spread in every portion of the north of that region but had crossed the Rhine.
>
> The two characteristics of these confederations, which now cover Europe like a network, are war against property and hatred of the Semitic revelation. These are the legacies of their founders; a proprietary despoiled and the servants of altars that have been overthrown. Alone, the secret societies can disturb, but they cannot control, Europe. Acting in unison with a great popular

movement they may destroy society, as they did at the end of the last century. The French disturbance of '48 was not a great popular movement. It was a discontent which required nothing more for its solution than a change of ministry: but the sovereign and his subjects were in sudden confusion; the secret associations are always vigilant and always prepared; they took society by surprise, but having nothing really to rely upon except their own resources, the movement however disastrous has been an abortion.

It is the manoeuvres of these men, who are striking at property and Christ, which the good people of this country, who are so accumulative and so religious, recognize and applaud as the progress of the liberal cause. (B. Disraeli, *Lord George Bentinck: A political biography*, London 1852, pp. 553–4. Quoted in J. M. Roberts, *The Mythology of the Secret Societies*, Paladin, 1974, pp. 20–1.)

The notion of the 'enemy within', of secret (and not so secret) societies and organizations conspiring to overthrow the fabric of society is still present in the second half of the twentieth century. It is however rather an easy way out to blame something uncomfortable or unpleasant on the machinations of evil men acting together in secret. Furthermore, quite how, during a revolution, these secret societies succeed in bringing thousands on to the streets, into the anarchic sections (of revolutionary Paris) and soviets (of revolutionary Russia), how they succeed in totally undermining the police and soldiers who would normally suppress such disturbances, and so on, has never been explained by holders of the conspiracy theory.

Of course secret revolutionary societies have existed. They were particularly active in Europe in the years immediately after the fall of Napoleon. But, as J. M. Roberts has shown, probably the most significant thing about these societies was the mythology which surrounded them. Governments feared that these societies could create, if not revolution, then at least serious trouble; and the societies themselves, encouraged by the fears of the authorities, began to believe that they were in reality capable of overthrowing the restoration regimes.

However, while you would be hard put to it to find any revolution conceived and executed by a dedicated band of conspirators, it is possible for relatively small groups of men with clear ideas – who possibly met together in secret and/or indulged in political agitation before the revolution – to attempt to take over and direct a revolution once it has begun. Lenin and the Bolsheviks are the obvious example here; they certainly were not a secret society who conspired to 'cause' or 'start' the Russian Revolution.

Agitation by such a group – subversion if you like – by means of the printed or the spoken word may also contribute to the undermining of the existing regime. But such attacks on the old regime are not necessarily the work of dedicated revolutionaries. Before the French Revolution of 1789 and the Russian Revolution of 1917 criticism of the ruling regime did not centre on revolutionary bodies, but on influential groups within society. In France it was the aristocracy, jealous of its own position in the face of increased royal authority and a growing royal bureaucracy, which introduced the notions of equality, freedom and rights into political debate, especially in the years 1787 to 1789. In Russia the creation of *zemstvos* (roughly equivalent to elected county councils whose electors needed substantial property to qualify for the franchise) in 1864 gave the gentry and the intelligentsia a focus for political activity. It was then possible for them to argue that, if they were permitted elective authorities for local government, why could they not elect a national assembly? By the beginning of the twentieth century even conservative members of the Russian gentry were sympathetic to such an idea. Charles I's alienation of a large part of Parliament, and the British government's alienation of a large part of the commercial interest in the American colonies can be seen as fitting into a similar pattern. Whether such a pattern can be discerned in Europe before 1848 is something for you to decide as a result of this course.

(b) A revolutionary ideology

The question of ideology as a cause of revolutions ties in closely with the preceding discussion. The French aristocracy and the Russian *zemstvos* obviously had ideas about how government and society should function, but in neither case was there a single set of ideas agreed upon unanimously by the individuals involved. Furthermore these ideas alone cannot be said to have caused the revolutions. The Jacobins of the Year II simply did not exist as a body of any sort before 1789; the Bolsheviks certainly had an ideology, but this in no way can be said to have caused the revolution of February 1917. I think it might be reasonable to say that in the period immediately before a revolution there is considerable intellectual ferment and debate over systems of government and the order of society; and that ideologies come to the fore and become real issues *after* the collapse of the old regime and during the struggle by Amann's 'power blocs'.

(c) A rising class

You have almost certainly come across the proposition that revolutions are caused when a new, influential and powerful class in society demands a position in government corresponding to its new economic pre-eminence. Generally the proposition is stated in economic terms and as such it stems from the view developed by Karl Marx that societies are essentially structured around their modes and levels of economic production. The great models demonstrating this theory of the causes of revolutions were the English Revolution of the 1640s and the French Revolution of 1789; revolutions in which, it was held, a rising class, the bourgeoisie, overthrew the old ruling class, the nobility, and the old infrastructure of society, feudalism, was replaced by the new, capitalism. But considerable research has subsequently been done on early seventeenth-century England and late eighteenth-century France, and I think that it would probably be difficult to find any modern historian who now subscribed whole-heartedly and uncritically to such a simple interpretation. Yet the interpretation is far from being dead, indeed many historians do accept the broad view that feudalism was replaced by capitalism, and of these, many think of themselves as Marxists.

You will study Marx's ideas about his interpretations of the events of 1848 in detail in Part II. Briefly, I think it is worth saying here that Marx did not regard the revolutions as anything approaching those of England in the 1640s and France in the decade after 1789. These two earlier revolutions had, he believed, transformed the economic and social structures of the societies involved; but the actual political action of overthrowing the existing governments in these revolutions was merely the consolidation or the immediate precursor of social and economic change. In his *Contribution to the Critique of Hegel's Philosophy of Right* (1843–1844) Marx noted that there could also be 'a partial, *merely* political revolution which leaves the pillars of the building standing'.[6] Yet Marx saw classes involved even in such 'merely political' revolutions as the title of his pamphlet *The Class Struggles in France: 1848 to 1850* suggests. Marx was not alone in seeing class struggles as a significant element in the revolutions of 1848. The other great interpreter of the events in France during 1848, Alexis de Tocqueville (who you will also study in Part II), wrote of the violent June Days in Paris that:

[6] Quoted in Kumar, op. cit., p. 100.

In truth it was not a political struggle (in the sense in which we have used the word 'political' up to now) but a class struggle, a sort of 'Servile War' . . .

One should note, too, that this terrible insurrection was not the work of a certain number of conspirators, but was a revolt of one whole section of the population against another . . . (Alexis de Tocqueville, *Recollections*, trans. G. Lawrence, ed. J. P. Mayer and A. P. Kerr, Doubleday and Co., 1971, p. 169 and p. 170. Set book.)

You don't have to subscribe to any kind of Marxist ideology to recognize that 'classes' in the modern social sense of the word, were developing and were noted to be developing in mid-nineteenth century Europe. To what extent a class struggle caused the revolutions of 1848, and to what extent Amann's 'power blocs' correspond to social classes during these revolutions is clearly a question for you to keep uppermost in your mind during the course.

(d) Repression creating discontent

Of course repression can create discontent among those people who are being repressed, but it does not necessarily bring people out on to the streets to overthrow the old order or to create new and rival power blocs. Repressive governments can be highly efficient in their repression; Stalin's Russia and Hitler's Germany are obvious twentieth-century examples. For the moment I think that there are two significant things worth noting about repression on the eve of a revolution:

(i) it has probably helped create discontent among a large enough section of the population to make them react positively and significantly against it, and

(ii) probably more important, the repressive forces are either not sufficient to cope with the disorder, are reluctant to cope, or are given no orders and refuse to act on their own.

(e) Economic disruption creating discontent

Both the French Revolution of 1789 and the Russian Revolution of 1917 coincided with severe economic distress among the lower classes of society. But, of course, there can be severe economic distress which leads to popular disturbances, but not to revolution. A brief look at the social history of eighteenth-century England reveals scores of disturbances brought about by high prices, but even though the situation reached serious proportions in, for example, 1766 and in 1795 and 1796, there was no revolution. Trotsky noted that 'the mere existence of privations is not enough to cause an insurrection; if it were, the masses would always be in revolt'.[7] Furthermore famine and privation were not present on a similar scale in England or America on the eve of their revolutions.

However, historians and sociologists can still argue for a link between the economic situation in a country and a revolution. Basically their argument is that revolutions have occurred during a period of economic change when expectations are mounting and have been rudely interrupted by a recession, possibly even an economic crisis. In the case of America it was not so much recession as the new policies of the British government which hindered and limited the expectations of the colonial merchants who led the initial campaign in the run up to the war and revolution.

The proposition that revolutions occur in a generally improving situation, or a situation in which expectations have been raised, is not new and it is worth quoting at length here the conclusions which Tocqueville reached on this

[7] Quoted in Crane Brinton, *The Anatomy of Revolution*, Vintage Books, 1965, p. 33.

subject in his study of France on the eve of the Revolution of 1789 – conclusions which relate to my brief note above on 'repression' as much as to economic distress.

> . . . it was precisely in those parts of France where there had been most improvement [in the standard of living in the peasantry] that popular discontent ran highest. This may seem illogical – but all history is full of such paradoxes. For it is not always when things are going from bad to worse that revolutions break out. On the contrary, it oftener happens that when a people which has put up with an oppressive rule over a long period without protest suddenly finds the government relaxing its pressure, it takes up arms against it. Thus the social order overthrown by a revolution is almost always better than the one immediately preceding it, and experience teaches us that, generally speaking, the most perilous moment for a bad government is one when it seeks to mend its ways. Only consummate statecraft can enable a King to save his throne when after a long spell of oppressive rule he sets to improving the lot of his subjects. Patiently endured so long as it seemed beyond redress, a grievance comes to appear intolerable once the possibility of removing it crosses men's minds. For the mere fact that certain abuses have been remedied draws attention to the others and they now appear more galling; people may suffer less, but their sensibility is exacerbated. At the height of its power feudalism did not inspire so much hatred as it did on the eve of its eclipse. In the reign of Louis XVI the most trivial pinpricks of arbitrary power caused more resentment than the thoroughgoing despotism of Louis XIV. (Alexis de Tocqueville, *The Ancien Régime and the French Revolution*, trans. Stuart Gilbert, Collins/Fontana Library 1966, p. 196.)

(f) Serious divisions within the old regime and disintegration of government
I have already touched on this 'cause' in (a) – mentioning the hostility to the old regime centring on influential elements in the old society – and (d) – mentioning the old regime's inability to rely on its forces of repression at the crucial moment.

In a commonly quoted passage Lenin concluded that the 'fundamental law' of revolution,

> which has been confirmed by all revolutions, and particularly by all three Russian revolutions in the twentieth century, is as follows. It is not enough for revolution that the exploited and oppressed masses should understand the impossibility of living in the old way and demand changes; it is essential for revolution that the exploiters should not be able to live and rule in the old way. Only when the '*lower classes*' *do not want* the old way, and when the 'upper classes' *cannot carry on in the old way* – only then can revolution triumph. This truth may be expressed in other words: revolution is impossible without a nation-wide crisis (affecting both the exploited and the exploiters).

> It follows that for revolution it is essential, first, that a majority of the workers (or at least a majority of the class-conscious, thinking, politically active workers) should fully understand that revolution is necessary and be ready to sacrifice their lives for it; secondly, that the ruling classes should be passing through a governmental crisis, which draws even the most backward masses into politics (a symptom of every real revolution is a rapid, tenfold and even hundredfold increase in the number of members of the working and oppressed masses – hitherto apathetic – who are capable of waging the political struggle), weakens the government and makes it possible for the revolutionaries to overthrow it rapidly. (V. I. Lenin, *Left Wing Communism, an Infantile Disorder*, quoted in Kumar, op. cit. pp. 160–1. It is also quoted and analysed at length in Dunn, op. cit. pp. 13–15.)

It is not necessary to accept the underlying ideology of this passage to acknowledge that the suggestions in it, even if not a 'fundamental law', contain an element of possibility. Historians and political scientists with political opinions widely different from those of Lenin have made similar assessments.

14

In *The Anatomy of Revolution* in which he compared the English, the American, the French and the Russian Revolutions, Crane Brinton noted that 'the ruling classes in our [old regime] societies seem, and not simply *a posteriori* because they were in fact overthrown, to have been unsuccessful in fulfilling their functions'. This lack of success was particularly marked in the Russian and French examples.

> The Russians here provide us with a *locus classicus*. To judge from what appears of them in print, Russian aristocrats for decades before 1917 had been in the habit of bemoaning the futility of life, the backwardness of Russia, the Slavic sorrows of their condition. No doubt this is an exaggeration. But clearly many of the Russian ruling classes had an uneasy feeling that their privileges would not last. Many of them, like Tolstoy, went over to the other side. Others turned liberal, and began that process of granting concessions here and withdrawing them there that we have already noticed in France. Even in court circles, it was quite the fashion by 1916 to ridicule the Czar and his intimates . . .

> Russia remains the classic instance of an inept ruling class, but France is almost as good a cause. The salons in which the old regime was torn apart – verbally, of course – were often presided over by noblewomen and attended by noblemen. Princes of the blood royal became freemasons, and if they did not quite plot the overthrow of all decency, at least sought to improve themselves out of their privileges and rank. Perhaps nowhere better than in France is to be seen one of the concomitants of the kind of disintegration of the ruling class we have been discussing. This is the deliberate espousal by members of the ruling class of the cause of discontented or repressed classes – upperdogs voluntarily siding with underdogs. (Brinton, op. cit., pp. 51, 52 and 53.)

Hannah Arendt made the point that,

> Generally speaking, we may say that no revolution is even possible where the authority of the body politic is truly intact, and this means under modern conditions, where the armed forces can be trusted to obey the civil authorities. Revolutions always appear to succeed with amazing ease in their initial stage, and the reason is that the men who make them first only pick up the power of a regime in plain disintegration; they are the consequences but never the causes of the downfall of political authority. (Hannah Arendt, *On Revolution*, Penguin, 1973. pp. 115–16.)

Finally Kumar observed similarly that

> If we look at the *anciens régimes* of the various Revolutions, the striking thing is the extent to which the ruling authorities have already lost effective political control over their subjects. Sovereignty is an empty legal formula, in the conditions of such societies. . . .

> Groups at all levels of society are struggling to make ground, exploiting the political vacuum which is often not consciously noticed, and certainly not intended by any particular group. (Kumar, op. cit., p. 41.)

The six 'causes' which I have discussed in this section are not, of course, to be taken either singly, or together as 'fundamental laws' governing what circumstances cause, or do not cause revolutions. I have relied heavily on the conclusions reached by historians and political scientists who have mainly concerned themselves with comparative studies of the English, the American, the French and the Russian revolutions. With regard to the revolutions of 1848, and this course in particular, the 'causes' which I have described are designed for you to use as guides for the kind of questions to ask about these revolutions: to what extent had Louis-Philippe's regime collapsed in February 1848, for example; to what extent had economic and social expectations increased in Italy in the years before 1848, and so on. It may be that some of these 'causes' have little or no relevance to some of the revolutions. Finally, of course, general 'causes' should not be confused with the occasion of the different outbreaks. While the underlying causes which generated the revolutions may be similar there is no reason to suppose that the occasion which brought crowds on to the streets of Vienna in March 1848 was necessarily similar to the occasion which brought crowds onto the streets of Berlin about one week later.

1.2.4 THE COURSE OF REVOLUTIONS

Comparing the French Revolution between 1789 and 1799 with that of 1848 and 1852, Karl Marx wrote that history repeats itself 'the first time as tragedy, the second as farce'.[8] While not necessarily agreeing with this theatrical metaphor, many historians and social scientists have been tempted to discern a pattern in revolutions – a 'natural history' of revolutions. Brinton concluded that 'it is . . . approximately true to say that power passes on from Right to Left until it reaches a limit short of the most extreme or lunatic Left'.[9] The pattern of this movement, roughly follows a traditional course: pre-revolutionary tension; the collapse of the old regime; the rule of the moderates; the overthrow of the moderates by the radicals; the reign of terror; the thermidorean reaction (Thermidor being the month of the revolutionary calendar during which Robespierre was overthrown); a military dictatorship; and finally some kind of 'restoration'. Thus Robert V. Daniels could write in his account of the Russian Revolution that during the terror and the civil war in Russia 'the parallel with the English Puritans and with the Jacobins in France is dramatically apparent'. Then, by 1921 the Bolsheviks' policies had alienated many of the people who had initially supported revolution.

> The 'Workers' Opposition', on the far left of the Communist Party, corresponded to the left-wing Hébertist faction among the Jacobins, or to the socialist seats such as the Diggers and the Levellers in revolutionary England . . .
>
> Lenin's master stroke at this point, viewed in the perspective of revolutionary history, was to carry out his own 'Thermidor'. He proclaimed the New Economic Policy, and with it an end to the effort to reconstruct Russian society overnight . . .
>
> The Workers' Opposition was denounced as 'petty-bourgeois anarchist deviation', condemned and broken up; it shared the fate of earlier idealist hold-outs, like Babeuf in France and Lilburne in England . . .
>
> The differences between Stalin and Bonaparte are obvious, but the analogy is none the less remarkable. Both imposed themselves on their respective nations at corresponding stages of the revolutionary process; both demanded and got the release of tremendous national energy. (Robert V. Daniels, 'The Russian Revolution runs its course', in Heinz Lubasz (ed.) *Revolution in Modern European History*, Macmillan, 1966, pp. 129, 130, 131 and 133.)[10]

But also, Daniels goes on to argue that 'without much stretch of the imagination, the new ideas and policies of Stalinism can readily be viewed as aspects of a "restoration"'.

This pattern has not been applied simply to the great revolutions. One historian has investigated the 'logic' of Brinton's book with reference to the seventeenth-

---

[8] Karl Marx, 'The Eighteenth Brumaire of Louis Napoleon' in Marx, *Surveys from Exile*, Penguin, 1973, p. 146. Set book.

[9] Brinton, op. cit., p. 254.

[10] Daniel's essay is extracted from his book *The Nature of Communism*, Random House, 1962.

century revolt in the Netherlands.[11] Nor is the model for this pattern in revolutions of recent construction. Its foundation was laid by Hegel early in the nineteenth century; his analysis of the French Revolutions was the first important theoretical framework of the course of revolutions and it profoundly influenced Marx's interpretation of 1848. The great nineteenth-century Swiss historian Jacob Burckhardt (1818–1897), a student of Ranke, detected a terrifying acceleration of the 'historical process' during a revolutionary crisis. 'Developments which otherwise take centuries seem to flit by like phantoms in months or weeks, and are fulfilled . . . '[12] While probably few historians now would subscribe whole-heartedly to Burckhardt's belief in a strict 'historical process', or to cycles in history, his pattern of revolution is basically that repeated by historians who subscribe to the 'natural history' theory of revolutions.

I don't want to go into the debate here about whether or not there is a pattern in the course of revolutions. The 'natural history' school has not gone un-challenged. It has been criticized as quite irrelevant to any useful study of the French Revolution of 1830.[13] To quote Kumar again:

> While the general agreement on the stages of revolution is impressive, the explanatory accounts given are usually less so. There is not much serious analysis of the 'causal mechanics' of the process, the forces that propel the revolution, with apparent irresistibility, from one stage to another . . .
>
> There is simply a description, in temporal order of a series of events occurring over a certain period of time. The illusion of an explanation is created by references to 'the dialectic of revolution', 'the inherent logic of revolution', or to some ill-defined psychological properties of crowds and masses. But what links up the stages of a revolution into the widely-observed uniformities remains mysterious. An identical weakness of logic was largely responsible for discrediting nineteenth-century theories of social evolution, with their fondness for postulating stages of human development without explaining how societies moved from one stage to another. The sceptical attitude commonly held towards theories of revolution no doubt stems partly from seeing the parallel. (Kumar, op. cit., pp. 75–6.)

However, while not going into the debate on patterns in revolutions in any detail, I think that it is worth pointing out that participants in revolutions have often seen patterns and have looked to past events to guide their actions. Hannah Arendt noted that

> while the part played by the professional revolutionist in the outbreak of revolution has usually been insignificant to the point of non-existence, his influence upon the actual course a revolution will take has proved to be very great. And since he spent his apprenticeship in the school of past revolutions, he will invariably exert this influence not in favour of the new and the un-expected, but in favour of some action which remains in accordance with the past. Since it is his very task to assure the continuity of revolution, he will be inclined to argue in terms of historical precedents, and the conscious and pernicious imitation of past events, which we mentioned earlier, lies, partially at least, in the very nature of his profession. Long before the professional revolutionists had found in Marxism their official guide to the interpretation

[11] G. Nadel, 'The Logic of *The Anatomy of Revolution* with reference to the Netherlands revolt', *Comparative Studies in Society and History*, 1960, pp. 452–84. Nadel actually demonstrates that the simple mechanical application of the 'logic' of a model is self defeating.

[12] Jacob Burckhardt, *Reflections on History*, English edn., London, 1943, quoted in Kumar, op. cit., p. 221.

[13] J. Rule and C. Tilly, '1830 and the unnatural history of revolution', *Journal of Social Issues*, 1972, pp. 49–76. The same point was made by Clive Church in a paper, 'Models of Revolution and their Application to the European Revolutions of 1830 – A Preliminary Exploration', read at the British Sociological Association's History and Sociology Study Group, held at Warwick in November 1973.

and annotation of all history, past, present and future, Tocqueville, in 1848, could already note: 'The imitation [i.e. of 1789 by the revolutionary Assembly] was so manifest that it concealed the terrible originality of the facts; I continually had the impression they were engaged in play-acting the French Revolution far more than continuing it'. And again, during the Parisian Commune of 1871, on which Marx and Marxists had no influence whatsoever, at least one of the new magazines, *Le Père Duchêne*, adopted the old revolutionary calendar's names for the months of the year. (Arendt, op. cit., pp. 260–1.)[14]

When Lenin arrived at St Petersburg in his sealed train in April 1917 he was greeted by a band playing *La Marseillaise*. A modern historian has written of the 'tyranny' of the Parisian examples of revolution over the revolutionaries in St Petersburg (Petrograd);[15] many of the Russian revolutionaries saw themselves cast in moulds first made during the 1790s and they constantly feared the Thermidorean reaction which appeared to them certain to come simply because it had come in France.[16]

Working through this course you may find if helpful to break up the 1848 revolutions under headings derived from the natural history model as I have roughly outlined it; obviously though, you will have to ensure that you never distort the course of any one revolution trying to make it fit the model. The question of the extent to which revolutionaries in 1848 did imitate the past is one that will recur throughout the course, and it is a question worth keeping in mind as you work through the units.

1.2.5 PARTICIPANTS

One of the main topics running through this course is 'who participated in the revolutions?' I mentioned above that both Marx and Tocqueville wrote of 'class struggles', but it is worth noting here, at the very beginning of the course, exactly what social groups or classes were present in mid-nineteenth century Europe to participate in these struggles.

Exercise

Two questions now which I think you should be able to answer from your basic historical knowledge.

1 Which class (or social group, if you prefer) was present in enormous numbers in early nineteenth century Europe which is hardly present at all in modern Europe?

2 What sort of class (or social group) was just beginning to appear as a result of the economic changes in early nineteenth century Europe?

Discussion

● The groups or classes which I wanted you to pick out were (1) the peasantry and (2) an industrial working class.

---

[14] Incidentally the 'new' magazine which Arendt mentions being published during the 1871 Commune, *Le Père Duchêne*, took its name from Hébert's radical journal published from 1790 to 1794. There was also a *Père Duchesne* in 1848, and a Bonapartist *Petit Fils du Père Duchesne*.

[15] John Keep, '1917: The Tyranny of Paris over Petrograd', *Soviet Studies*, vol. XX, 1969, pp. 22–35.

[16] For a brief description see Stephen F. Cohen, *Bukharin and the Bolshevik Revolution*, Wildwood House, 1974, especially pp. 131–2.

The size of these two groups in individual countries and the effect which they had upon the different revolutions will be dealt with subsequently by individual unit authors, but it is worth emphasizing a general point here. It is very easy to over-estimate the speed of industrialization during the industrial revolution and to ignore

(a) that most Europeans in the middle of the nineteenth century were still very close to the land and a very high percentage worked on it

(b) that a very small percentage of Europeans worked in large factory units or with machinery which was the result of the new industrialization

(c) that, generally speaking, in urban areas small workshop units consisting of a master and his few journeymen still tended to predominate.

In Paris in 1848 there were still only about five workers to every one employer. In Britain, 'the first industrial nation' and the country which had more cities with a population over 100,000 than anywhere else in Europe (see Table 1), the 1851 census revealed that a quarter of all men over twenty still got their living from agriculture. The census also revealed that there were more shoe-makers than either coalminers or woollen workers, more blacksmiths than men who made iron, and as many domestic servants as workers in cottons, woollens and silks combined.

Table 1   The largest cities in Britain and France c. 1850 (population given in thousands)

Britain		France	
London	2,685	Paris	1,053
Liverpool	376	Marseilles	195
Glasgow	345	Lyon	177
Manchester	303		
Birmingham	233		
Edinburgh	194		

(The population of Britain (excluding Ireland) was 20.8 millions, the population of France was 35.8 millions.) ●

There is one final point that I want to make in this introduction about 'participants' in the revolutions of 1848. The revolutions witnessed mass crowd action and street fighting. You have probably come across descriptions of revolutionary crowds like that given by Edmund Burke in his *Reflections on the Revolutions in France*: 'a band of cruel ruffians and assassins, reeking with . . . blood'.[17] Similar comments have been made about the forces opposing in-surrection, such as this, from Raymond Postgate's account of the June Days in Paris in 1848:

> Arranged against them the proletariat found the National Guard, the Garde Mobile – a terrible organization, the 'élite of the slums drilled for butchery', which excelled in brutality – the whole of the army, and the forces of the Government. (R. W. Postgate, *Revolution: from 1789 to 1906*, Harper and Row, 1962, p. 179.)

Of course a revolutionary crowd, or a counter-insurgency force, is hardly likely to be an attractive body to those on the receiving end of its violence, or to those contemporaries or historians sympathetic to those on the receiving end. Sufficient work has now been done on the insurrectionary crowds of the

[17] Edmund Burke, *Reflections on the Revolution in France*, Everyman's Library no. 460, p. 68.

eighteenth and early nineteenth centuries for the notions of these crowds being made up of ruffians, pickpockets and, generally speaking, the very dregs of society to be dispelled.[18] It is, of course, probable that some such individuals did get involved with revolutionary crowds. Similarly, almost certainly, some 'ruffians' and some 'dregs' from the 'slums' found their way into the counter insurgency forces, but this does not justify a blanket assertion that such forces, or all of one particular part of them, were 'ruffians' or 'bullies'. It is, I think, rather too easy to put down examples of brutality and excessive violence in a revolution to the sadism of the perpetrators. The reasons are, almost certainly, far more complex, rooted in a variety of social, regional and economic differences between the combatants; furthermore, it is at least arguable that the heat of the moment and the passions aroused during a revolutionary upheaval can themselves prompt combatants to acts which they would not normally commit.

1.3 SOCIAL SCIENTIFIC APPROACHES TO REVOLUTION

The aim of this section is to acquaint you with some of the attempts made within the broad area of Social Science, (i.e. Politics, Economics, Sociology, Social/Psychology) to describe, explain and possibly predict the outbreaks of revolutions. Those of you who have never studied any Social Science before may find it difficult to grasp some of the concepts in this section on a first reading. If so, there is no need to worry; however I hope that some acquaintance with these theories will suggest additional insights to you in your historical examination of the revolutions of 1848. If you do experience difficulty, the five points which I have summarized at the end of the section (p. 30) will help you form a clear idea of the concepts being used here.

1.3.1 SOME INITIAL PROBLEMS

The study of revolution is beginning to emerge as a systematically investigated field within the social sciences, involving serious efforts to develop a general theory that will account for the data collected mainly by historians, provide an explanation of why revolutions do or do not occur and possibly enable social scientists to make predictions about the likelihood of revolutions under specified conditions.[19] But there is no theory of revolution within present day social sciences, only materials and models. A theory of revolution presupposes a fully developed theory of society which can account for change and historical development. At the present state of social science such a theory cannot be expected, because of departmentalization and specialization between the disciplines which work against a synthesis. The attempts to develop the Marxist framework to fit developments in capitalist societies have, to my mind, not yet provided a sufficient basis for the examination of revolutionary conditions.

I think that the basic problem inhibiting an adequate understanding of the revolutionary process is the fact that a revolutionary situation has to be seen as a complex combination of two types of conditions:

---

[18] The best introduction, if you wish to follow this up, is George Rudé, *The Crowd in History, 1730–1848* John Wiley, 1964, which incidentally contains a chapter on the French crowds in 1848.

[19] For a good study of recent scholarship see Isaac Kramnick, 'Reflections on Revolutions: Definition and Explanation in Recent Scholarship', *History and Theory*, XI, i, pp. 26–63.

1   The objective or structural conditions, i.e. the distribution of power based on the control of production and distribution, and the precipitating conditions such as economic crises, or the inability of a government to govern – in short the contradictions between various subsystems of society.

2   The subjective conditions, the political beliefs or consciousness of various sections of the population, their readiness for action – a growing antagonism and polarization between 'topdog' and 'underdog' groups.

Despite the recent predominance of psychological approaches, the second line of inquiry has shown very little progress. The aspect mostly in need of examination is the way objective realities come to be perceived subjectively by those groups participating in revolutions. The analysts have grouped themselves into those adhering to a notion of 'spontaneous consciousness', where the consciousness rises directly out of the objective situation, and those adhering to a 'subjectivist' notion who tend to neglect the objective situation.

The whole issue revolves around the question of the 'agent' of revolution, which groups or class will carry through the transformation of society: the industrial working class, the peasant classes (in the Third World) or the *Lumpenproletariat*, those groups that are completely excluded from society. Marx saw the working class in its totality as the historical agent of revolution. Lenin shifted his focus to the party as the decisive element and as the vanguard of the working class. Mao Tse-tung adapted Marxism 'creatively to the Chinese situation' by realizing the revolutionary potential of the peasantry. The Cuban theory of revolution recognizes the *guerilla-foco* as the historical subject by virtue of his consciousness, whereas certain theoreticians of the 'New Left' in industrialized countries have directed their attention to marginal groups within society as well as to the intelligentsia. I think this development indicates that the traditional class analysis is an important, but not the only aspect of revolution, and cannot fully explain all revolutionary processes in their structural roots and class focus.

There is obviously a problem of objectivity in the study of revolution and Clive Emsley has already drawn your attention to John Dunn's remarks about the impossibility of being neutral. The theorists I mentioned in my preceding paragraph were all revolutionary activists whose writings were action-orientated and whose criteria of justification would be practical political success. Social scientists studying revolution aim to be objective and explanatory. However social scientists are involved in the argument whether their research *can* be objective and value-free (in the way that natural scientists approach their field of study as neutral observers), or whether the selection of a topic and the research methods employed, necessarily involve valuation and consequently ideological bias. It has been argued recently[20] (forcefully and, in my opinion, successfully) that main-stream American social science at least, expounds the very fallacy it attributes to the activists, since so much of its work implies obvious value commitments – mostly expressed in attempts to give counsel on how to avoid or repress revolutionary outbreaks.[21]

[20] Sheldon S. Wolin, 'The Politics of the Study of Revolution', *Comparative Politics*, vol. 5, no. 3.

[21] See, for example, 'Project Camelot' designed by the American government during the 1960s to find ways of preventing revolutions in the Third World. I. L. Horowitz (ed.) *The Rise and Fall of Project Camelot*, M.I.T., 1967.

Defining the object of study – the concept – is already part of the analysis and explanation of the concept. This is especially true of an historical concept like that of revolution which is imbued with so many symbols and meanings. In this section I want to start by pointing to two aspects of recent social scientific literature which 'deviate' from traditional studies of revolution. First, I think that such studies tend to ignore the unequal distribution of, and access to, centre positions within societies as a fundamental reason for attacks against existing societal orders.[22] Secondly this type of literature precludes the possibility of regarding revolutions as a form of social and political change. Instead, revolutions are categorized as specific cases of collective violence and instability of political systems. I believe that there has been an obvious shift of focus to the analysis of societal aggression and the use of violence as the primary concern in the recent proliferation of studies in revolution.

Chalmers Johnson, whose model I will discuss later, regards violence as the overriding concept, defining revolution consequently as 'purposive political violence', that is, the use of violence 'in order to cause the system to change'.[23] Harry Eckstein proceeds in a similar way by defining revolution as 'internal war', which 'denotes any resort to violence within a political order to change its constitution, rulers or policies'.[24] Raymond Tanter and Manus Midlarsky regard the degree and duration of violence as the vital factor.[25] Ted Gurr, who presents us with the most systematic study of 'turmoil', 'conspiracy' and 'internal war' (including revolutions), considers the common denominator of these events to be political violence, by which he means 'all collective attacks within a political community against the political regime, its actors . . . or its policies'.[26] Analysing revolutions from this angle implies, to my mind, specific preconceived notions which tend to obscure the fact that violence is not confined to revolutions or riots. As early as 1917 Max Weber suggested that the ultimate definition of a modern state was that it held the monopoly of the legitimate use of physical force within a given territory.[27] In the modern era it is governments who have employed force with the greatest intensity and destructiveness.[28] However the debate among sociologists as to whether society depends on 'consensus' or 'coercion' is still the centre of conflict analysis, and whichever side you take leads to a different approach to the study of revolution. A further point which links, albeit tenuously, with the question of violence, is that political scientists tend often to regard revolution as an abstract, without relating it to the social and historical contexts of specific revolutions. The definitions of Amman and Tilly discussed above by Clive Emsley, and the concept of revolution employed by Harold D. Lasswell and A. Kaplan in their study *Power and Society*,[29] seem to me to represent a rather one-sided power-political standpoint. By reducing revolution to a problem of changes in power

[22] One can divide societies generally into *centre* and *periphery* according to the control of resources, power of decision making, etc. *Societal* – inferred from society, meaning all aspects of human interaction within society.

[23] Chalmers Johnson, *Revolutionary Change*, Little, Brown, 1966.

[24] Harry Eckstein, 'On the Etiology of Internal War', *History and Theory*, Vol. 4, 2, p. 133; also: 'Introduction, Towards the Theoretical Study of Internal War', *Internal War*, Free Press, 1969, p. 1.

[25] Raymond Tanter and Manus Midlarksy, 'A Theory of Revolution', *Journal of Conflict Resolution*, vol. 11, no. 3, p. 168.

[26] Ted Robert Gurr, *Why Men Rebel*, Princeton University Press, 1970, p. 2.

[27] Weber's definition is quoted in Paul G. Lewis and David C. Potter (eds.) *The Practice of Comparative Politics*, Longman, 1973, pp. 16–17. D231 set book.

[28] Barrington Moore, *The Social Origins of Dictatorship and Democracy*, Allen Lane, 1973, p. 505.

[29] Harold D. Lasswell and A. Kaplan, *Power and Society: A Framework for Political Analysis*, Yale University Press, 1952.

they prevent a deeper analysis of the structural causes and process of revolutions.

My own definition of political revolution would be: the attempt of social groups, which had been more or less completely and permanently excluded from positions of dominance within the state, to redistribute – unilaterally or with the help of segments of the ruling groups – incumbent positions in order to lay the foundation for new effective criteria for the access of political power. Non-revolutionary change, consequently, is constituted by the redefinition of criteria through bargaining processes between 'centre' and 'periphery', i.e. privileged and deprived social groups. Revolutionary change then means sudden fundamental change, a 'qualitative leap' prepared by a quantitative, gradual development.

There is a further factor which I believe to be of crucial importance for the definition of revolution: not only the degree of change is decisive but also the direction it takes. Thus I would distinguish – and in this point I seem to diverge from Clive Emsley's definition – between *progressive* political change, where the criteria, collectively redefined, entail a greater participation of groups in political decision-making, and the obvious counterpart of *regressive* political change. The concept of revolution creates that of counter-revolution. The latter can be seen as a sudden overthrow of the political order without opening up a perspective to large social groups that were hitherto excluded from exercising greater political influence. Counter-revolutions have the function of holding the 'tide of emancipation' that was slowly created within the old order. Despite their often populist appeals, like that of National Socialism in Germany or Fascism in Italy, I do not consider they invoke fundamental, structural changes, but rather that they retain the same socio-economic base. (Those of you who have taken the A301 course, *War and Society*, will notice that my definitions of revolution and counter-revolution leads me to differ from Professor Alan Milward who argues that National Socialism was a revolutionary movement.)[30]

3.3   COMPARATIVE HISTORICAL APPROACHES

Comparative historical approaches offer sets of assertions about the causes and course of revolutionary change, on the basis of the detailed knowledge of the authors about some of the great revolutions. The studies by Crane Brinton[31] and Lyford Edwards[32] can be seen as first attempts to establish an empirical social scientific science of revolutions. Crane Brinton summarizes his inquiry into the outbreak of revolutions by noting five recurring causes: (1) societies are in a state of economic improvement; and the revolutionary movement is carried by those dominated groups that profit from the economic prosperity. (2) Every revolution is based on a strong class antagonism between those who occupy the dominant positions in society and those who are denied access to power; the antagonism increases as the economic gap between the groups narrows. (3) The transfer of the allegiance of the intellectuals away from the established order. (4) The impotence of the governmental apparatus. (5) A gradual destruction of the old elites, whose members start to mistrust each other, lose their faith in the tradition of their own class and become involved in radical intellectual or humanitarian pursuits.

[30] A301 War and Society, op. cit., Unit 21, *Germany and World War II* especially pp. 10–11.

[31] Crane Brinton, *The Anatomy of Revolution*, op. cit.

[32] Lyford Edwards, *The Natural History of Revolution*, University of Chicago Press, 1927.

Exercise

Clive Emsley has already quoted substantially from Brinton's *The Anatomy of Revolution* in which the English, French, American and Russian Revolutions are compared. I accept that many of you will not have done any social science, but can you think of any criticisms which an empirical social scientist might level against Brinton's 'anatomy'?

Discussion

● There are four basic criticisms; I think that you might get the first two, but probably you are not likely to get the third and fourth without a reading of the comparative approaches in question.

1 It is questionable whether such a small number of case studies (only four, remember) can justify the far reaching conclusions which Brinton, and others, tend to put upon them.

2 The isolation of heterogeneous factors does not yet constitute a theory of revolution since nothing is really said about their inter-relationship.

3 There is no differentiation between those conditions which initiate the development of a revolutionary situation and those leading to the actual attempt to overthrow the government in power.

4 These studies focus more on dominated groups than on the incumbents of power positions.●

1.3.4 SOCIAL-PSYCHOLOGICAL THEORIES

These theories begin with the almost common-sense premise that discontent is the root of revolutions, and that it depends on 'the general mood in society' whether revolutions occur. As the explanation of revolutionary conflict depends on a specific kind of mediation between objective, societal or structural factors and the existence of a revolutionary consciousness, these theories represent an important step towards an adequate understanding of the phenomenon under scrutiny. The principal proponents are James C. Davies, R. Tanter and M. Midlarsky, Ivo and Rosalind Feierabend and Ted Gurr.[33] Davies attributes revolutionary conflict to prolonged periods of rising economic prosperity followed by a period of sharp reversal, which he calls the 'J-curve', i.e. the graphic representation of economic development.

The gap between expectation and gratification widens and becomes intolerable and the resulting frustration seeks outlet in violent action. 'If the frustration is sufficiently widespread, intense and focused on government, the violence will become a revolution . . .'[34]

It remains to explain why economic growth followed by an abrupt depression should create a revolutionary potential. For Davies it is obviously not economic growth as such that represents a destabilizing factor, but only the specific sequence of prosperity and depression. Thus the emphasis is on the construction of a social-psychological model, applied previously by Daniel Lerner in his

---

[33] James Davies, 'Towards a Theory of Revolution', *American Sociological Review*, 1962. Rosalind and Ivo Feierabend, 'Aggressive Behaviour within Polities 1948–62', *Journal of Conflict Resolution*, 1966, pp. 249–271.

[34] Davies, op. cit., p. 547.

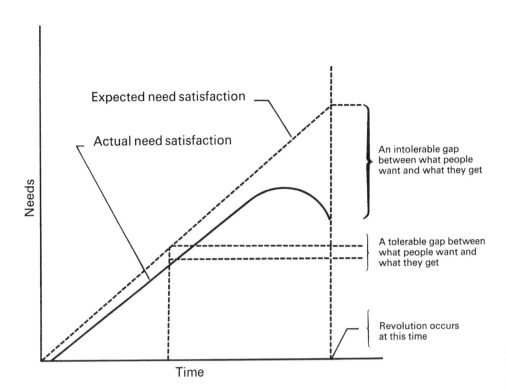

Expected need satisfaction

Actual need satisfaction

Needs

Time

An intolerable gap
between what people
want and what they get

A tolerable gap between
what people want and
what they get

Revolution occurs
at this time

Fig. 1
Davies 'J-curve' illustrating
need satisfaction and
revolution

study of social modernization.[35] Pulling the main argument together, we can say that this approach assumes a specific relationship between expected need satisfaction (these needs range from simple physical existence to complex social needs), actual need satisfaction and the anticipation of an increasing discrepancy between expectation and fulfilment. The explanatory power is based on the following deliberations: economic growth leads to satisfaction with those achievements already realized, but it also breeds the expectation of the continued ability to satisfy growing needs in the future. There is always a gap between actual and expected satisfaction, but this is regarded as 'normal' and thus tolerable. But the sudden reversal in economic development creates a greater gap and the assumption of growing losses. This anticipation produces a 'collective mentality' characterized by fear and frustration, inducing large segments of the population to revolt against existing circumstances.

The first general criticism of this theory concerns the obvious minimizing of the destabilizing consequences of economic *growth*. It is possibly not satisfactory to describe the relationship of economic growth to political change as a source for satisfying collective needs and as a motor for collective dreams or aspirations. It might be more fruitful to regard economic growth as the cause of the appearance of certain conflict groups within society: first, those groups which are favoured by the economic growth but who regard the absence or slowness in the redistribution of social prestige and political participation as unjust; and second, those groups who lose as a consequence of economic change – in contrast to the new winners or traditional dominant groups.[36] Thus, as Kumar describes it:

[35] Daniel Lerner, 'Modernization: Social Aspects', *International Encyclopedia of Social Sciences*, Vol. 10, pp. 392–3.

[36] cf. Manur Olson, Jr., 'Rapid Growth as a Destabilizing Force', *Journal of Economic History*, Vol. 23, 4, pp. 529–52.

Revolutions then are fed by the discontent of both the losers and the gainers in a period of rapid economic and social change. The gainers want to go on gaining and are impatient with any checks, human or natural, to their continued advance. They may also be driven by a desire to even up their rankings on the different social dimensions, for the economically advancing this means gaining social and political power. (Kumar, op. cit. p. 47).

The dissatisfaction of losers and new gainers can, as indicated above, be turned into collective violence. The possibility, however, that destabilizing factors of economic growth will not immediately bring the downfall or restructuring of an authority structure can be explained by referring to the fact that the surplus produced by economic growth increases the means of social control in the hand of the 'centre', social control that is based on normative, utilitarian and coercive assets. These means help to channel dissent with, for example, the help of a compensatory ideology.[37] Thus the arrival of a sharp depression reduces the surplus value of a society to a great degree, affecting the possibility of subsequent social control for the incumbents of dominant positions.

Secondly, it remains a problem to determine what intensity and duration of depression is required to produce a revolution. From the social-psychological standpoint one would have had to expect revolutionary change in the USA in the 1930s, disregarding the social-control factors at that time.

In his extensive study of collective violence in the world from 1961–65, Ted Gurr tackled some of the questions which Davies left aside, such as what factors determine the intensity of relative deprivation and its scope, in other words, what section of the population are likely to feel deprived and may become involved in revolt. His study – although a valuable contribution – shows to my mind, all the signs and shortcomings of so called 'positivist' and inductive social science, which by dissecting social reality into seemingly independent parts, does not see the 'totality' of human social experience. Ted Gurr's version of the premise of discontent is that the potential for collective violence in a nation or smaller community varies with the intensity and scope of socially induced discontent among its members. It is essentially a generalization of the 'frustration–aggression' hypothesis[38] from the individual to the social level. In trying to answer what kind of social conditions and processes of change raise discontent beyond the threshold of overt aggression, he delineates three lines of inquiry:

1   What are the psychological and social sources of the potential for collective violence?

2   What determines the extent to which this potential is directed against the political system, that is, to what extent is it politicized?

3   What societal conditions determine the scope and form of violence?

Basically, Gurr's theory is a social-psychological one, as psychological factors provide the causal link between societal variables, i.e. social, cultural, or economic variables and the outbreak of political violence. It is not objective deprivation, but relative deprivation, i.e. the 'perceived discrepancy between men's value expectations and their value capabilities'. 'Value expectations are the goods and conditions of life to which people believe they are rightfully entitled. Value capabilities are the goods and conditions they think they are

[37] The example of 'compensatory ideology' has been illustrated by Jurgen Habermas, *Technik und Wissenchaft als Ideologie*, Frankfurt, 1968, and Herbert Marcuse, *One Dimensional Man*, Abacus, 1972.

[38] The frustration–aggression hypothesis claims that any intervention with goal-directed behaviour (purposeful activity) will lead to frustration.

capable of attaining or maintaining *given the social means available to them.*'[39] Gurr, remaining throughout his book at this 'upper layer' of perception or consciousness, does not get down to a discussion of concrete social conditions, which is, I think, one of the greatest shortcomings of his study.

The greater the intensity of discontent, Gurr argues, the more likely is violence. The impulse to act, to revolt

> is determined by men's beliefs about the sources of deprivation, and about the normative and utilitarian justifiability of violent action directed at the agents responsible for it. Furthermore, societal variables that affect the focussing of discontent on political objects include the extent of cultural and subcultural sanctions for overt aggression, the extent and degree of success of past political violence, the articulation and dissemination of symbolic appeals justifying violence, the legitimacy of the political system, and the kinds of responses it makes and has made to relative deprivation. (Gurr, op. cit., p. 13.)

Gurr makes an attempt to specify why certain groups in society feel deprived at what times. The first relevant factor is the determination of the intensity of deprivation: the saliency of values and which kind of values. Based on the monumental field study by Cantril[40] – a cross-cultural survey 'of human concerns' – Gurr finds out which classes of human values are most salient in what population and in which subsection of these societies. 836 million people were questioned in Cantril's study; 55 per cent of their most valued assets were material values. Gurr tried further to determine the scope of relative deprivation in relation to the distribution of salience of values. Thus he identified a set of socio-economic strata for societies 'in the middle stages of economic development'[41] and related these findings to the specific value-hierarchies of the defined groups. It is obvious that everything depends on the identification of these groups and the means by which their value-hierarchies are established. Furthermore, from an 'objectivistic viewpoint', it seems doubtful whether questionnaires are the best way of establishing values or interest which are not purely dependent on the predominant ideology of the system. Gurr claims to have specified a

> set of variables that determine the potential for collective violence in any group at any time. The potential would be greatest in a nation most of whose citizens felt sharply deprived with respect to their most deeply valued goals, had individually and collectively exhausted the constructive means open to them to attain those goals and lacked any non-violent opportunity to act on their anger. (Gurr, op. cit., p. 85.)

So Parisian workers in 1848, Mexican peasants in 1910, the German *Kleinbürgertum* in the early 1920s, Hungarians in 1956, black South Africans in the 1960s fall into this category.

The most crucial question of course is why expectations rise. Gurr names the 'demonstration effect', coming from outside or inside, the 'rise of ideologies', which however is never sufficient in itself, and 'value disequilibria'. This last factor has been rather popular as an explanatory factor as it combines psychological with structural factors. I referred to the same phenomenon above by showing the destabilizing impact of economic growth. Rank disequilibriation, as Johan Galtung calls it, is the main factor in explaining aggression, or rather 'drives towards change', whether among individuals, groups or nations.

---

[39] Gurr, op. cit., p. 13.
[40] Hadley Cantril, *The Pattern of Human Concern*, Rutgers University Press, 1965.
[41] Gurr, op. cit., p. 85.

Prerequisites are inequal distribution of resources and the motivation towards upward mobility.

This theorem repeats, in a more stringent sociological way, what has been postulated before by de Tocqueville, Davies and to some extent Marx. Galtung suggests that if a person, group or nation experiences disequilibrium – in relation to the generally accepted value-structure of society/the international system – he will be 'constantly reminded of his objective state of disequilibrium by the differential treatment he is exposed to. This will force *a correspondence between his objective situation and his subjective perception* of it'.[42] Disequilibriated groups can be divided into 'overachievers' and 'underachievers', the 'gainers' and 'losers' who will necessarily react differently to their situation of imbalance. Although Galtung remains very much in the realm of positivist theory, he does recognize the fact that the 'overachiever' or the original 'underdog' who has climbed one step in the hierarchy may not only fight for the achievement of a complete 'topdog' position but may have to fight for the complete redefinition of at least some of the accepted societal values.

1.3.5 SYSTEMIC APPROACHES

Regarding the relatively weak explanatory values of those theories and categorizations mentioned above, it becomes clear that it is absolutely necessary to formulate a comprehensive theory of social change, which demonstrates the structural context for the conditions of the occurrence of societal crises as well as the strategic elements that determine the course of such an event.

Marx's studies of historical development and social change are particularly relevant in this case but as Unit 7 deals with Marx's analysis of 1848 I am not including the Marxist analysis here. It is necessary to stress, however, that all studies of revolution in this century are to a great extent influenced by Marx – even to the extent that they vehemently reject the basic Marxist premises.

Chalmers Johnson's studies represent one such systematic attempt to explain revolutionary change.[43] To understand why revolutions occur, 'we must have a knowledge of how and why the social barriers against violence have collapsed or have been breached'. The focus is the social system, which according to Johnson is 'any group of variables which are so arranged that they form a whole . . . and which . . . are mutually influencing ("interdependent") and . . . tend to maintain the relationship they have with each other over time ("equilibrium")'.[44] The basic premise of this 'structural-functional' approach is the existence of some form of moral community among members based on shared values, thus this way of looking at society assumes the validity of a consensus-theory of social integration.[45]

Johnson detects two necessary causes of revolutionary change: 'power deflation' and 'loss of authority'. The concept of power deflation refers to the image of power as 'political currency', i.e. as a medium of interaction, similar to the function of money in the economy. By virtue of a general confidence in the validity of such 'political currency' people give their support to a political regime. The deflation of power denotes the loss of this confidence and hence a

---

[42] Johan Galtung, 'A Structural Theory of Aggression', *Journal of Peace Research*, 1964, p. 99.

[43] Johnson, op. cit., and *Revolution and the Social System*, Hoover Institute Press, 1964.

[44] Johnson, 1966, op. cit., p. 3.

[45] I have already noted the dichotomy between the so-called 'consensus-theory' and 'coercion-theory' of society.

withdrawal of voluntary support. The logical consequence would be the increase
in coercion as a substitute for support. In the end deterrence becomes the only
basis of social integration. Confidence in the system and its regime is a sign for
a 'system in equilibrium', whereas power deflation leads to a disequilibriated
system' and carries with it the potential for revolutionary change. The second
condition, that of a 'loss of authority', is a result of unsuccessful attempts by the
élites or leaders to 're-synchronize' value structures (norms, ideologies etc.), or
the failure of the process of social adaptation to changes in the environment.
At this stage the use of force is no longer legitimate and with the loss of the
means of coercion (the final 'accelerating' condition) the time is ripe for
revolution.

Johnson summarized the factors leading to an unbalanced social system under
four headings:

1   Sources of value change located within the social system: including changes
'brought about as a result of intellectual developments and the acceptance of
creative innovations',[46] or, alternatively, the replacement of, for example,
religious authorities by secular monarchs.

2   Sources of value change located outside the system, that is in the international arena (as a consequence of war or new developments in communica-
tion) which create new 'reference groups' or other changes in social values.

3   Sources of environmental change located within the system and tech-
nological innovations.

4   Sources of environmental change from outside the system: for example, the
transfer of technology to underdeveloped countries, or the effects of foreign
trade and international migration.

The main purpose of the social system, as seen from this perspective, is to
persist. Social change can either be channelled to enforce the system or else its
destabilizing effect will cause a breakdown. The reference to or rather the
implicit analogy with the system of organisms (i.e. the idea of change through
'homeostasis' which implies the maintenance of the internal structure and the
successful passive adaptation to outward pressure), shows, I think, the con-
servatism of this approach. Society is basically 'a collectivity of people who
share certain values which legitimize the inequalities of social organization and
cause people to accept them as morally justified'.[47] Hence, whenever an
imbalance is caused within the system it is important 'to realize the creative
potentialities of political organization' as Johnson is convinced 'that revolution
is always avoidable' if the realization succeeds.[48]

Systemic theoretical approaches to society are, I think, no substitute for a
theory of society since they are always based on a particular understanding of
social reality. Consequently the attempts either to maintain or restructure a
system have to be seen as related to particular interests present within the very
structure of society. Looking at the recent attempts by social scientists to explain
the phenomenon of revolution there is a detectable shift in the underlying
value-premise from 'pro-establishment' to 'pro-underdog'.

A crucial element in the social psychological studies was the subjective definition
of interest groups revolting against society. Gurr, for example, sees conflict as
the incompatibility of the actors' subjectively defined goals. In this case the

[46] Johnson, op. cit., p. 65.
[47] Ibid, p. 19.
[48] Ibid, p. xiv.

resolution of a conflict is possible by changing or manipulating those values and goals. As such a settlement is compatible with the situation of a high degree of social injustice and repression, it is therefore necessary to differentiate between this definition of a subjective interest and that of an objective interest. Thus conflict can be seen alternatively as a structurally induced incompatibility of interests; that is, it arises out of the structural relationship between groups in society of which people may, or may not, be aware. These 'objective' interests then are analytically, and very often in reality, different from overt expressions of what people want.

Gurr's study is merely concerned with the subjective side of interests without regard for deeper lying structural antagonisms within a society. The crucial task is therefore to identify the structural-objective interests of the élites or topdogs in maintaining a specific authority structure and also those of the 'underdogs' in attempting to realize alternative structures. The essential question consequently becomes: to what extent are disadvantages and privileges within a society structurally induced? Such an enquiry is identical with Johan Galtung's analysis of 'structural violence' in a system. Galtung introduced this concept in order to show the inadequacy of the concept of 'peace' as the absence of collective violence.[49] As such a negative definition of peace can entail a highly repressive, but nevertheless stable order, 'peace', in its positive sense, has to be seen not only as the absence of overt violence but also as the absence of a much more pervasive kind of violence which is often called 'social' or 'structural' violence.

1.3.6 SOME SUGGESTIONS FOR THE COURSE

In this section of the unit I have tried to outline briefly some of the theories put forward by social scientists about revolutions; I have also criticized each theory so that you will not regard any single one as definitive. In conclusion I would like to suggest how I think you might use some of these theories to ask questions of the historical material on 1848 which you will work on during this course.

1 You will have noticed that I do not regard the comparative studies which have been done on revolution very highly but
    (a) Brinton's five causes give you five useful ways to start investigating the causes of the revolutions of 1848.
    (b) in this course you are undertaking a comparative study yourself; the point is that all of the revolutions you are studying occurred in the same year and comparison and contrast could be more valuable because of the limited time-scale.

2 What was the role of economic forces in the revolutions? Was there a period of prolonged economic prosperity followed by a period of sharp reversal in the societies experiencing revolution in 1848? Can we come to any conclusions about whether economic growth or economic depression caused a destabilizing in these societies? (Davies.)

3 Is there any perceived discrepancy between value expectations and value capabilities in prompting revolutionary violence in 1848? How was any such discontent channelled into political action? (Gurr.)

4 Were there sources of 'value change' or 'environmental change' producing unbalanced social systems in 1848? To what extent can we talk of 'power deflation' and 'loss of authority'? (Johnson.)

[49] Johan Galtung, 'Violence, Peace and Peace Research', *Journal of Peace Research*, 1969, pp. 167–99.

5 Can the application of the concept of structural violence to the societies of 1848 lead to a greater understanding of the growth of revolutionary forces? Does this 'objectivist' concept relate with Gurr's 'subjectivist' concept of relative deprivation if you equate 'structural violence' with 'objective deprivation'?

1.4 HISTORIANS AND THE REVOLUTIONS OF 1848

In all the history courses, or history components of courses, at the Open University we have emphasized that history itself does not *say* anything. Historians communicate their interpretation of historical data; the personal nature of this interpretation and the fragmentary nature of the available data leads different men to different conclusions, and thence to controversies. The history of the revolutions of 1848 is no exception to this. Earlier in this unit I quoted John Dunn's assertion that the value-free study of revolution is impossible. Furthermore there were two significant elements present within the revolutions of 1848 about which it is difficult, some would say impossible, to be neutral: militant nationalism and militant socialism. The personal attitude of the historian of the revolutions of 1848 to these issues will probably colour his interpretation of the events.

I want you now to turn to your set book, Melvin Kranzberg, *1848: A Turning Point?* This is a collection of articles and excerpts from books relating to the revolutions of 1848. The book itself is not new (it was first published in 1959) and you will see that most of the articles and excerpts in the book date from around the centenary of the revolutions. Some of the controversies in the book have become less immediate in historical circles now, and some of the assertions have been amplified or corrected by more recent research. Nevertheless the book provides a valuable introduction to the revolutions and to different historical interpretations of them.

Would you now start your reading of Kranzberg's book? I will suggest questions about particular issues raised in some of these papers as you work your way through.

First read Bernadotte E. Schmitt's paper (pp. 1–9). This gives a brief introductory outline of the events of 1848. Also, since it was written in 1948, it can be said to set the scene for most of the other papers in the collection.

Exercise
When you have read Schmitt answer the following questions:

1 What do you think Schmitt is trying to do in this paper?

2 What effect does this have on the paper? (You may find it helpful to read my discussion of the first question before tackling this.)

Discussion
● 1 Schmitt believes that by and large as the revolutions failed they might be better termed 'revolts' (something else for you to think about given the definitions above in 1.2.2). He goes on to show what effect this failure had on the subsequent history of Europe and he emphasizes throughout that many of the principal problems of Europe in 1848 were still present and, in many respects, little changed in 1948.

2 You have probably heard it said that every age writes its own history. Schmitt sets out specifically to look at 1848 from the viewpoint of 1948 and this, I think, dates his paper considerably since the way he raises several issues is possibly more illuminating about attitudes in 1948 than about the actual effects of the revolutions of 1848 on subsequent European history. With the smugness of hindsight we know that General de Gaulle did eventually become ruler of France and that he left a constitution giving vast powers to the president of the republic which, while not ensuring a *balance* between executive and legislature, did give some stability and not just under the General himself (see Schmitt's statements on p. 3). Schmitt's question about whether Austria is capable of a truly independent existence (p. 5) might seem curious today; so, after 1956 in Hungary and 1968 in Czechoslovakia, might his belief that the problem of central Europe had been solved 'temporarily' by Soviet power (p. 7). Finally, given the serious political and economic instability of Italy in the late 1960s and early 1970s it is curious again to find Schmitt concluding that Italy 'has perhaps come nearer to establishing a firm national state on a democratic basis than any of the other countries involved in the revolutions of 1848' (p. 8).●

Exercise

Now read the two papers on France by Lord Elton (pp. 9–16) and by J. P. T. Bury (pp. 17–23), and answer the following question. Would you say that the difference between Elton and Bury was fundamental or simply one of emphasis?

Discussion

● I think that the difference between Elton and Bury is largely one of emphasis. Given what they set out to do in their respective books this is hardly surprising. Elton's book, from which Kranzberg extracted the passage which you have just read, is called *The Revolutionary Idea in France 1789–1871*; Bury's book, on the other hand, is a straightforward narrative of French history from 1814–1940. It is therefore more likely that Elton would emphasize revolutionary ideas as seen in his contrast between the 'old' and the 'new' revolution in greater detail than Bury. Even so Bury's assertion that

> The great drama of 1848 lies in the conflict between those who want to seize the opportunity to solve the social problem by radical reforms of the conditions of labour and those who are determined to resist social changes which they fear will lead to chaos and anarchy (p.18).

is very close to Elton.●

However the virtual agreement between Elton and Bury over the Revolution of 1848 in France does not mean that there is no longer controversy, or that Elton and Bury wrote definitive accounts. Let's look more closely at the June Days in Paris. The following passage comes from George Rudé's *The Crowd in History: 1730 to 1848*. Read it, then answer the questions which follow.

> The conflict was certainly not one between factory workers and their employers: this would have been impossible in the circumstances of the time. Paris, as we have seen, was still a city of small workshops and crafts that had little changed, in this respect, since the first great revolution of 1789. If we examine the occupations of the 11,693 persons who were charged in the affair, we find a remarkable similarity to the trades of those who stormed the Bastille and captured the Tuileries sixty years before. We find among them no fewer than 554 stonemasons, 510 joiners, 416 shoemakers, 321 cabinet makers, 286 tailors, 285 locksmiths, 283 painters, 140 carpenters, 187 turners, 119 jewelers, and 191 wine merchants; and most of these occupations are among the dozen largest

categories to which the prisoners belonged. It is even likely – though here the evidence is not precise enough to be conclusive – that among these prisoners, small masters, shopkeepers, and independent craftsmen outnumbered wage earners, possibly by as much as two to one. Rémi Gossez, a French historian who has studied the question far more deeply than any other, adds the point that, because of the government's pre-disposition to consider all *hommes en blouse* as potential rebels, the proportion of workers among those arrested and released was considerably higher than among the smaller number of those actually convicted. Moreover, he goes on to show that there was no clear-cut class division between the two opposing forces: workers served in the National Guard alongside property owners, shopkeepers, clerks, and professional men; the Mobile Guard was largely composed of young workers, many of whom had fought on the barricades in February; and, of industrial employers, most remained neutral in the fighting in order to guard their factories and shops, while several fought with their employees in the insurgents' ranks. From this he concludes that, while the social conflict was genuine enough, it was one that ranged small producers, lodgers and sub-tenants (and not only wage earners) against shopkeepers and merchants, and against landlords and 'principal' tenants (often shopkeepers), rather than against factory owners, masters, and industrial employers.

Such points are worthy of attention, and they suggest that in some respects at least the June insurrection looks back to older forms of social protest by small consumers and producers that we have noted in earlier chapters. Striking as certain of the similarities between the crowds in 1789 and June 1848 are, however, the differences are equally great. In the first place, in the earlier revolution, the initiative was generally taken by the workshop masters, who were more literate and more highly politically educated than their apprentices and journeymen, and the traditional crafts played the major role in popular insurrection. This time the case was somewhat different. The initial impetus, as we have seen, came from the workers in the national workshops: this in itself was something new, as when similar workshops were closed down in Paris in 1789 and again in 1791 it hardly caused a ripple in the struggle of the political parties. Yet, in June, it was only a minority of the workshop workers that took part: a fact due, no doubt, to the government's decision to continue paying wages even after the fighting had begun. The backbone of the insurrection came from other groups. Thus building workers account for the largest category of those arrested; and it was noted that each of the main centres of resistance was held by its own distinctive trade association: carters at La Villette, coal heavers and dockers along the St. Martin canal, bronze workers on the Boulevard du Temple, and joiners and cabinet makers in the Faubourg St. Antoine. But even more significant: industrial development, though slow and thinly spread, had brought in railways and the beginnings of mechanized industry and among the arrested insurgents, alongside the joiners, cabinet makers and locksmiths of the older crafts and shops, we find the names of some 80 railwaymen and 257 *mécaniciens*. It was the workers in the railway workshops of La Chapelle, already a thriving industrial suburb to the north of the old city, who built some of the first barricades in the Faubourg Poissonnière; and we find railwaymen also joining port and riverside workers in manning the barricades on the Island of the Cité. These workers had since February been among the most highly organized and militant in the capital; Gossez describes them as forming 'the vanguard of the insurrection.' (G. Rudé, op. cit., p. 175–7.)

Exercise

1   How does this passage alter the impression of the insurgents of the June Days given by Elton and Bury?

2   As a result of the research into the composition of the insurgents do you think Elton and Bury's statements about the immediate cause of the June Days require some qualification?

Discussion

● 1   Elton described the June Days as a struggle between the Haves and Have-Nots. The occasion of the insurrection was the attempt to close down the

National Workshops and, he argues by implication, the insurgents were the workmen from these workshops refusing to disband (p. 15). Bury's description tallies with this: 'the men of the National Workshops, and the unemployed who had been refused admission to them, determined to resist the order for dissolution, and all the working-class quarters of Paris rose in sympathy with them' (p. 21).

However, Rudé's description of the insurgents shows that a large percentage came from the traditional trades of Paris with a stiffening of well-organized workers from the new industrial suburb of La Chapelle. There were, he notes, only 'a minority of [National] workshop workers'; probably the government's decision not to disband the Workshops and to continue paying the inmates during the insurrection kept the number of insurrectionists down. Rudé also suggests that there was no clear cut class division between the opposing combatants; incidentally, contrast what he says about the Mobile Guard with the quotation which I gave you from Postgate (see above, p. 19).

2   There is a very general point about history which arises out of this question and which I think is worth emphasizing: even the work of the greatest historians is likely to require substantial modification in the light of new research. The order to close the National Workshops may have sparked off the June Days, but since we now know that the majority of the insurgents came from the traditional trades and that the Workshops were kept going during the insurrection, we need to ask new questions about exactly why the insurrection occurred. Clearly it was not simply a case of the threatened closure of the Workshops leading all of the inmates to rise up in armed rebellion supported by the Parisian working class. For the fundamental causes of the June Days we have to go deeper into the French Revolution of 1848, something which we shall be doing in Part II.

One final point of controversy about the June Days which is worth raising here; a problem common to much social history when crowds and crowd action comes under scrutiny – how many insurgents were there?

(a) They may have numbered as many as 100,000. This, at least, was the number of muskets later seized in the insurgent districts.[50]

(b) General Cavaignac's estimate of their strength was 50,000, a figure likely to be high.[51]

(c) The numbers involved in the actual fighting must not be exaggerated; they were probably not more than 20,000, one in ten or less of the workers of Paris.[52]

Probably no research will ever solve this precisely.●

I want you to move on now to the next four papers in Kranzberg: those of A. J. P. Taylor (pp. 24–39), Veit Valentin (pp. 40–8), William Ebenstein (pp. 49–53) and Friedrich Meinecke (pp. 54–63). As you will see they all deal with the German lands in 1848 – perhaps it is no bad thing to have this emphasis here given the overall emphasis of this course towards France. Read the four papers and answer the following questions.

---

[50] Rudé, op. cit., p. 173.

[51] Robert W. Lougee, *Midcentury Revolution, 1848*, D. C. Heath and Co., 1972, p. 98.

[52] Alfred Cobban, *A History of Modern France*, Penguin, 1965, Vol. II, p. 144.

Exercise

1 What is the main controversy between the authors; is it one of emphasis or is it more fundamental?

2 Do you consider that any modern events influenced the authors of these papers, and if so what were they?

3 Can you see any problem for an historian in allowing himself to be influenced unduly by modern events?

Discussion

● All the papers agree that the German Liberals of 1848 were defeated. The controversies between them concern the activities of the Liberals during the revolution, and what happened to German liberalism after 1848.

If we start by contrasting Taylor with Valentin, I think you will find some agreement about the men in the Frankfurt Parliament; Taylor notes that they wanted to achieve German unity 'by persuasion' (p. 30) and that the majority, the moderate men, 'shrank from violence' (p. 37); Valentin notes that they wanted to be just to everyone (p. 46) and that they took no action to remove their enemies (pp. 44–5). But while Valentin emphasizes the 'passionate heroism' of the German revolutionaries, Taylor is critical of them for sacrificing liberalism 'to the national cause' (p. 31). There is an even wider divergence of opinion over what happened to German liberalism after 1848. According to Taylor the Liberals counted for less and less and finally for nothing at all (p. 38). Valentin seems to agree that in politics the moderates became impotent (p. 42), but he believes that the spirit of the liberal revolution and in particular the 'purity' of its 'patriotism' lived on; he regards this spirit as being present in 1866 (when the Prussian victory over Austria in the Austro-Prussian War brought German unity closer), the year overshadowed by the 'brilliance and fulfilment' (p. 47) of 1870–1871 (when victory over France in the Franco-Prussian War united Germany under the Prussian Crown). 'Brilliance and fulfilment' are the last words Taylor would juxtapose in his assessment of German unification.[53]

There is similar agreement and controversy when Ebenstein and Meinecke are brought into the debate. Ebenstein concludes that the Liberals were defeated because they were forced to fight a war on two fronts, against the feudal Junkers and absolute monarchs on the one hand and against the working class on the other (p. 51). Meinecke takes a rather similar line (see especially his concluding paragraph p. 63). But Meinecke, like Valentin, emphasizes the 'all-pervading spirit of idealism' (p. 57) among the liberal revolutionaries, an emphasis totally lacking in Ebenstein who appears, in his conclusion, to criticize the Germans for allowing liberal democracy to fail in contrast with other countries which made successful revolutions (pp. 52–3).

Questions can be raised about each of these interpretations. Taylor and Ebenstein are, at least by implication, critical of the German Liberals for their

[53] In fact in *The Course of German History*, Hamish Hamilton, 1945, Taylor concluded of 1866 that 'in short, Germany was conquered not united' (p. 109). Of the final unification in 1871 he wrote: 'The Bismarckian Reich was a dictatorship imposed on the conflicting forces not an agreement between them. The parties did not compromise; they were manipulated by Bismarck – pushed down when they threatened to become strong, helped up when they appeared weak ... [Bismarck] had defeated liberalism; therefore the Junkers accepted him despite the national Germany he had forced on them. He had united Germany; therefore the middle classes accepted him despite the defeat of liberalism' (pp. 115–16).

failure; in a sense their analysis of the situation can be taken to suggest that the Liberals had no chance in the first place being the very men that they were and given the forces arranged against them. Valentin mildly rebukes the Liberals for not taking action against their enemies; yet from Taylor's analysis you could well ask what action the Liberals could have taken. Karl Marx hit the nail on the head with an article in his newspaper the *Neue Rheinische Zeitung* in early June 1848:

> The Assembly in Frankfurt performs parliamentary exercises and lets the governments act. Even assuming that this learned council succeeds in contriving the best agenda and the best constitution, what use is the best agenda and the best constitution when in the meantime the governments have placed bayonets on the agenda. (Karl Marx, *The Revolutions of 1848*, Penguin, 1973, p.120.)

Valentin and Meinecke are sympathetic to the noble patriotism of 1848, but this sympathy skirts over the unsavoury side of the nationalism of 1848 with regard to the claims of certain national minorities – an aspect given full play by Taylor.

2 and 3 (I think that it makes more sense if I take my discussion of questions 2 and 3 together.) If you looked at the dates of the books from which these extracts were taken you might have concluded that the authors of all of them were writing under the shadow of Nazism and the Second World War, and also that their work reflected their own personal positions. Thus in a very simplistic sense Taylor and Ebenstein might be taken as attempting to explain the German 'problem' from the point of view of the winning side in the war; the climax towards which both the books work is the Nazi take-over and the Second World War – look again at Taylor's comment about German emigrants to the USA after 1848: 'the best of their race – the adventurous, the independent, the men who might have made Germany a free and civilized country . . . They, the best Germans, showed their opinion of Germany by leaving it for ever' (p. 38).

Valentin and Meinecke, both of whom fell foul of the Nazis, can be seen as defending the ideals of nineteenth-century German liberalism in the light of what happened subsequently. Yet this, at best, is a distortion; it would be an insult to any of these historians to suppose that they set out deliberately to write propaganda – and incidentally Valentin's book *Geschichte der deutschen Revolution von 1848–1849* (from which the translation *1848: Chapters of German History* comes) was first published in Berlin in two volumes dated 1930 and 1931 (before the Nazi take-over).

In the introduction to his book on the Frankfurt Parliament, Frank Eyck embarks on a discussion of the pitfalls in studying nineteenth-century German history which is worth quoting at some length.

> The historian is flattered by current political interest in his problems. Yet his task is made none the easier by it. The pages of history are not only a record of the past, but a guide for future action. The politically active have always looked to history for support in their political struggles. The official German school of historians after 1870 was not only concerned to justify the Bismarckian solution, but also to prevent a return to what it regarded as the confusion and lack of purpose of the Frankfurt Parliament. Anti-Bismarckian historians, on the other hand, have tried to discover as many positive achievements as possible at Frankfurt which could be used to mould Germany more to their liking. Indeed after what appeared to them as the interlude of the Bismarckian Reich, the founders of both the Weimar Republic and the Federal Republic had, in certain ways, to go back to 1848. Thus, too often, German history has been interpreted as a series of right and wrong turnings. This is understandable and almost inevitable with a country which has had as turbulent a history as

Germany. The question of what had gone wrong, between 1914 and 1918, between 1933 and 1945, was a powerful incentive to historical research. However stimulating, to pose the problems in this way is to invite difficulties. The texture of historical events is broken. The course of things is seen from one aspect only. Developments are selected which illustrate this particular side, others are omitted. The author is committed in advance to a certain position which deprives him of the freedom of movement every historian should have. He is defending one side, criticising the other, instead of being above both. In the concrete terms of the pre-Bismarckian period, these writers are bound to support all 'liberals' or 'progressives' against the 'reactionaries' who impeded progress. The liberals are the heroes. The reactionaries, with Metternich at their head, are the villains. Frederick William IV as a person, and the German Confederation as an institution, never leave the dock. These 'democratic' historians assume their guilt. Anything about the heroes which does not fit into the theory is quietly omitted.

To get away from this kind of approach is not as easy as it may appear. In Germany, historians have not unnaturally been sensitive to the effect their writings were likely to have on the political future of the country. At a time of rising National Socialist agitation before 1933, for instance, a historian who believed in the importance of preserving the Weimar Republic might well have felt that any exposure of liberal shortcomings in 1848 could do political harm. It is always more comfortable for the historian to be on the side of 'progress' than to expose himself to the accusation that he might have a blind spot for tyranny, and that he is insensitive to the sufferings of the persecuted and to the importance of human and political freedom. This risk will have to be taken. A sustained effort should be made to apply the same standards to all the parties involved, whether for or against freedom of speech. Those who opposed the immediate granting of all civil rights were not necessarily opposed to them in principle. Some of them might have judged that the time to grant them had not yet come. Many reforms have failed because they were forced through too quickly. This is a matter of historical fact and does not imply any lack of attachment to civil liberty on the part of the historian. While he may and perhaps ought to have his own views as to what form of government he may favour for a particular country *today*, he must not subject his historical vision to political and ideological blinkers. Whether immediately successful or not, every approach to the problems of 1848, from the extreme right to the extreme left, must be examined on its merits. Thus it will not do to regard as pure obstructionists those who insisted on maintaining the Austrian connection. This is done by many historians, supporting the exclusion of Austria from Germany, whether pro- or anti-Bismarck. If one side was entitled to its aims, so was the other. It is absurd to regard political agitation as honourable and high-minded if directed towards Prussian leadership and as an intrigue if opposed to it. (Frank Eyck, *The Frankfurt Parliament 1848–1849*, Macmillan, 1968, pp.1–3.)

Yet even if we remove the four papers on Germany in Kranzberg from the emotional context in which they were written, and even if we successfully remove our own 'political and ideological blinkers', there is no reason to suppose that the controversy over German nationalism and liberalism in 1848 will automatically be resolved.●

I want you now to read the remaining five papers in Kranzberg, those of Sir Lewis Namier (pp. 64–70), Hans Rothfels (pp. 71–9), G. P. Gooch (pp. 80–6), Priscilla Robertson (pp. 87–91), and Francois Fejtö (pp. 92–103). As you read through them I think that it would be well worth your while to note the salient points and the general line of interpretation. You will probably find it useful to refer back to any such notes as you progress through the course. Again in these papers you will find a predominance given to events in Germany and Austria. The differences in interpretation are obvious: Namier lines up with Taylor and Ebenstein; Rothfels with Valentin and Meinecke (I suspect that you will find it easier to grasp Rothfels' defence of the German Liberals than the defence put forward by his fellow countrymen earlier in the book). Robertson conflicts directly with Fejtö over whether there were any significant gains in European development as a result of the revolutions. At times the papers take each other up almost directly on particular issues which I think adds to the immediacy of the debate. Gooch draws up a balance sheet of the results in Germany and Austria, and on the credit side he records the abolition of serfdom in the Austrian lands (p. 86); Robertson asks whether this made up 'for the extra repression on all other Austrian subjects?' (p. 92). More important, Rothfels takes up the criticism of the German Liberals' nationalism as propounded by historians like Namier (whom he quotes), and argues that they have confused the nationalism of 1848 with the blatant aggressive manifestations of later generations (pp. 78–9). Whether in the long run you agree with Rothfels or not, or with the various 'isms' that will constantly occur in this course – liberalism, nationalism, communism, socialism – it is worth keeping in mind the point that political ideas and concepts are not constant from one generation to the next and do take on widely differing manifestations.

ACKNOWLEDGEMENTS

Grateful acknowledgement is made to the following for material used in this unit:

American Sociological Association for Figure 1 from J. C. Davies, 'Towards a theory of revolution', *American Sociological Review*, 27, No. 1, 1962; Macmillan, London and Basingstoke, and St. Martin's Press, New York for extract from Frank Eyck, *The Frankfurt Parliament: 1848–1849*, Macmillan 1968, reprinted by permission; John Wiley & Sons Inc. for extract from George Rudé, *The Crowd in History: 1730–1848*, copyright © 1964 John Wiley, reprinted by permission.

33/11